Seeing, hearing, taste, smell, touch—
You may not think about them much.
They're your FIVE SENSES and they do
Some super-duper things for you.

Learn about them and you'll say
One, Two, Three, Four, Five...

Hurray!

1

You see with your eyes.

2

You hear with your ears.

3

You taste with your tongue.

4

You smell with your nose.

5

You touch with your fingers and skin.

Seeing

Eyes will help you find your way
From home to school and back each day.
"The light is red," eyes tell your feet.
You better wait to cross the street!

Eyes let you see green grass, blue sky—
The fish that swim and birds that fly.
When you see candles on a cake,
You know you have a wish to make.

How many candles do you see on this cake?

Hearing

Ears hear what friends and family say
Or footsteps as they come your way,
Your cat's meow, your puppy's bark—
Your ears hear even when it's dark!

Ears hear that WHACK when ball meets bat.
A whispered secret? Your ears hear that!
Ears hear the pop of bubble gum
And the rat-tatta-tat of a beating drum.

A drum is loud. What are some other loud sounds?

Taste

Wouldn't it be a terrible waste,
To eat fresh corn you could not taste?
Your tongue's a detective — it sends you tips
About the foods that pass your lips.

Taste buds give your tongue the power
To know a lemon's very sour.
Pretzels are salty! Ice cream's sweet!
Your tongue tells you what's good to eat.

What are some other sour foods?

Smell

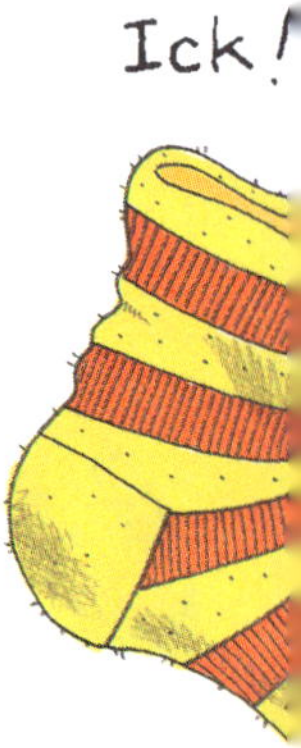

It whiffs. It sniffs. Kerchoo! It blows.
What lets you smell? Your nifty nose!
It tells you what the cook is making:
"That's an apple pie that's baking!"

Sour milk? Some stinky cheese?
Dirty socks? Ripe strawberries?
Is that a skunk? Is that a rose?
You'll get an answer from your nose.

What things smell good? What things smell bad?

Touch

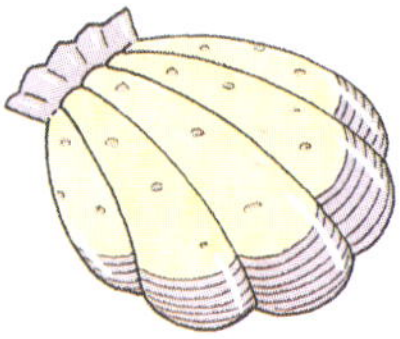

Your skin lets you know feathers tickle,
Wool is itchy, sharp thorns prickle.
Have you picked up a hot potato?
An ice cube? Or a squashed tomato?

Toes feel soft moss on the ground.
Hands know an apple's smooth and round.
Skin lets you feel a summer breeze
And says a teddy's nice to squeeze.

What other things feel soft?

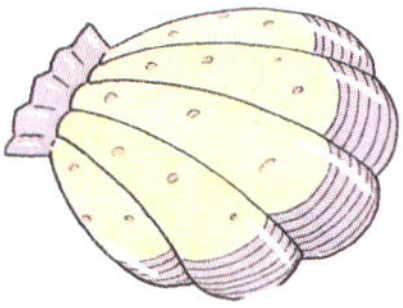

Now here's a game that's fun to play.
Let your five senses lead the way.
What is noisy? What is quiet?
What's so sweet you'd like to try it?
What is red? What is bright?
What is round and very light?

What is cold? What is hot?
What is soft and what is not?
What is bumpy? Can you tell?
What things have an awful smell?
What is wet and what is dry?
What might you see in the sky?

Hip - Hip - Hurray!

Seeing, hearing, taste, touch, smell —
That winning team that serves you well —
Deserves a cheer, so let's all say:
One, Two, Three, Four, Five...

Hurray!